Simply Us
Poetry from three generations…

Gale
Bernice
Gale

Written by:
Bernice Gale, Suzanne Gale
& Filisha Gale

Simply Our Thoughts
Poetry from three generations...

Contents

Dedication

First and foremost, we would like to thank God for blessing us with this passion, talent and for allowing us to share our work with others.

To the generations before and after us who have a love for writing and poetry.

To the ones we love, once loved, and lost. Through all our happiness and pain, we bring you not only our thoughts but also our feelings and experiences.

To all our readers we hope you enjoy our work and are able to walk away with something, whether it's hope, peace, or motivation. You are not alone in any struggle you face.

A Name

A name is to identify you and I.

We were brought up with it from a child.

It is with us in whatever we do.

It sticks to us just like glue.

If the names were mixed up for a day it would be a lot of confusion, wouldn't you say?

If you were called David as you go along, you would not even turn around.

If someone you loved in the state ecstasy called you someone else names unintentionally,

It would be a sad moment that is true because that is what a name is meant to you.

B. Gale

Father I Thank Thee

Father, I thank thee for giving me life.

For day and for night.

I thank thee for the birds that sing so bright.

And for the moon that shines its light at night.

Father, I thank thee for the sunshine, and for the sweet-smelling flowers and vines.

I thank thee for the waterfalls and streams that makes me feel like I'm living in a dream.

Father, I thank thee for the rain that vegetates our earth and for the creatures of the sea.

The animals that roam the jungle free.

Father, I thank thee for the trees and for the wind that blows a beautiful breeze.

Father, I thank thee for the food, veggies, and the fruits.

My family and my friends.

Father, I thank thee for loving me.

S. Gale

Elements of Art

We had many sessions in procession.

Art is cool, you could sit on a stool and create a pool.

What's your desire, red like fire?

There are no dimensions to arts intention.

Give specific examples and various art samples.

The element of design often intertwined with broad and thin lines.

Created are symbols and signs.

A mass volume of productions needed no introduction.

It's a process in molding, folding, even rolling.

A ball it may even appear big or small.

Penetrating, even regenerating?

The mind of the artist just keeps creating.

Symmetrical, Asymmetrical, it may seem technical.

Balance is a challenge to those that want harmony.

"Little", artist command feeling texture in their hands.

Bumpy, rough, even smooth, come take a ride in my prelude.

Space, not waste, everything in place to the artist liking and taste.

The End! In its evidence is created to "Self-expression."

S. Gale

Mechanical Bird

Take me on a flight over the sunset and into a space of nothingness, so I could look at the beauty of whiteness.

Let me imagine the illusion of flying, into the heavens and feel the spiritual connections with the Creator of the universe.

Glide me over the rivers and the water of the seas.

Travel to places unknown to others.

I want to see the beauty of nature below me to enjoy the creatures and animals of the jungles.

Learn the culture and the lives of people.

Mechanical bird fly high, fly low.

Take me to the wonders of the world, created for me to experience and explore.

S. Gale

Grey Hair

It sticks up in the air not giving a care who wants to stare.

Here, there, and everywhere.

You may dye, fry, press, or stick it.

Pluck, cut, or snip it.

Grey hair will be back in a minute.

You're reminded of it every day when you look in the mirror.

Take a wink or a blink and they're scattered like ink.

My friends, I'm telling you it's a losing battle too.

Grey is here to stay.

So, accept and respect that grey is boss, or you will always be at cost if you think they'll get lost.

We are all getting old and though we may not want to be told, grey hair will be BOLD.

So, don't be sad and blue just accept it as part of beautiful you.

S. Gale

Please Don't Love Me

Please don't love me; because I might commit myself to saying, "I do."

Please don't love me; so, I can get to know you through communication, understanding, trust, honesty, and respect.

Please don't love me; so, I can share with you, enjoyment, excitement, and pleasure.

Please don't love me; so, I can feel secure and show loyalty towards you.

Please don't love me; so, I can giggle "foolishly" and feel I've fallen in love.

Please don't love me; so, I can feel you're the best thing that ever happened to me.

Please don't love me; I don't want to hear of your sudden complaints of my faults.

Please don't love me; I don't want to feel the hurt and pain when you cheat on me and break my heart.

Please don't love me; I don't want us to be apart.

Please don't love me; because I don't want to hear "I don't love you."

Please don't love me; just be my friend.

S. Gale

Generation X

Dem' born without mind and soul.

No respect for the young and old.

Walking around without direction.

Clothes hanging off their midsection.

Bodies filled with tattoos and hole piercing.

No mind of thought.

No problem solved.

Guns and firearms are their first resort.

Life drop dead not a care in their head.

Step over you and walk to their crew.

What are we gonna do?

Life's human race is being a waste.

Generation X are preconception without direction.

S. Gale

Black Brothers

Black brothers, they are killing you one by one.

Black brothers, can't you see living in this evil society?

They are the authorities.

Your flesh and bones they'll crush like stones.

Your blood they'll watch run free.

They are your enemy.

Their hearts are filled with hate and jealousy.

You're not considered part of humanity.

They understand who you are, your soul is their ultimate goal.

Brothers, watch your back, you're under attack.

And that's a fact, just being BLACK.

S. Gale

Unconditional Love

I thought I knew what love was all about.

Possessiveness, jealousy along with physical violence, led to destruction.

I thought I knew what love was all about.

Attachment, insecurity, and fear.

Stunted an internal growth.

I thought I knew what love was all about, then I experienced unconditional love.

A love of freedom, total space, and growth.

A love that allowed me to open up my entire self.

Look at life - its views and issues with an open mind.

In turn, I was able to return that love that I learned.

Eliminating possessiveness, jealousy, and physical violence.

I experienced the joy and pleasures of expressing the whole "self."

I was given the space to find out who I am, what are my true values and beliefs.

I thought I knew what love was all about.

Now I do.

S. Gale

Pain

Pain, pain, pain, won't you go away.

Please go away, you make me feel so sad inside, so weak inside.

Please pain won't you go away; my heart feels so empty.

My eyes feel so sad.

Pain, won't you please go away?

Why do you control my body?

Making my mind feeling alienated from my body.

Why do you make me feel the anger that I do?

Pain, won't you go away?

Please go away!

I beg you so!

Why do you keep me silent for a long while, releasing the blood that thrust in my veins?

Why do you control me so, pain?

Exploding the anger within me that releases the silent pain?

Pain, why do you hold me?

Won't you just let me go?

S. Gale

Blessings

You say you want to be a blessed guest.

Get down on your chest breast.

Like the birds in the nest yes.

Consecrate and give your best yet.

To Him, you bring your request vest.

He'll fill up the rest.

Put away all your resentment, complaining you don't have a cent rent, and you're living in the basement of your friend Brent.

Worrying about when the month ends, if he'll put you out in a tent.

Feeling like sticking your head in a vent.

Beg, borrow, but never lend.

Generation curse devil got you in an outburst.

Like a dead man, you'll end up in a hearse.

Yo! Read the bible verse!

The quenching of your thirst.

Blessing is resting in the center of your turf.

Raise him, praise him, give him all he's worth.

S. Gale

Mother of The Village (Dedicated to Mrs. Shannon)

Your door was open wide for those of us that needed to come inside.

You were our voice so we would have a choice to make a difference in our lives.

Your ears never plugged up when others came to you with their problems and needed you to listen.

Your fridge was never empty when someone's belly was hungry.

Your bed was ready with comfort when someone needed a place to rest.

Your hands never collapsed when someone needed a hug.

Your house was full of laughter, joy, and love.

Endless days and nights you had to fight for what was right.

For sure you had sleepless nights.

You wanted unity in your community.

When others didn't care, you were there, talking the talk and walking the walk.

Mother of the Village, you never showed signs of fatigue or weakness.

You were our soldier mentally, emotionally, and physically strong.

Blessed with the gift of love and patience, you made a difference, touching the lives of so many.

S. Gale

Sun Knows No Color

Don't think because you're black!

From the beginning of time, the sun has been living for the earth.

As a major source, it meets our necessary needs.

Its life form brings us heat, light, energy, and joy.

We have taken it for granted to shine every day.

Enjoying all it has to offer.

Now we are destroying the earth that the sun lives for, causing it to retaliate burning through the ozone layer.

Human race, the sun knows no color.

Imagine the world without a sun.

What a cold world that would be.

S. Gale

Monserrat

Little island in the sun was once full of lushes, greens, and fun.

People young and old living together with one soul.

The year of '95. Who thought this would coincide, a monster big, a monster wide, would chase them to one side?

Everyone scattering running for their lives, not knowing whether they'll live or die.

Day suddenly turns to night, not being able to see a thing in sight, with many hearts living in fright.

Black in front and black in the back, the ashes build up in a stack.

Thousands fled abroad to a land that is new.

Looking back at loved ones sadden and blue.

A population of twelve thousand - eight thousand fled, nineteen dead.

Oh, island in the sun, your faith has just begun.

S. Gale

Birth of a Child

Legs opened wide for the world to see there's a life inside of me.

Painful as it may be, my family and friends helped me to push this new life into the world.

Sweating, screaming, squeezing, bloody body fluids, malfunctions running loose.

It's coming! Here it comes!

Little wrinkled and free.

It's a boy!

He cries so others are aware of his safe and alive arrival.

Baby, they call him.

Dependent on those that know him.

Nurturing, care, and food are vital to his survival.

Love is the key to his beauty.

His sense of awareness intact as he explores this planet know as earth.

S. Gale

Children

A beauty to look at.

They are true.

The mind of the child is developing rapidly to experience life in every possible form.

Free, spirited, fearless of the challenges in life.

The innocence of the child is to be seen and appreciated.

Their little hearts crave for joy and happiness, filling them with laughter.

Emotionally they are dependent on our love.

When I sit back and look at the children I see adults in small frames.

I smile, "they are the love of my life."

S. Gale

Body Language

Sitting on the subway looking all around.

Noticing the expressions of the faces traveling to places.

Many different nations, a gesture, a stare, even a frown.

Their body language speaks, sparking a curiosity in me.

Silent voices inside their minds thinking many thoughts.

I look and smile my body language has spoken.

S. Gale

Tattoos

You too picture view, various colors mixed for fun.

Tattoo, on the run.

Ink print skin deep, tattoo one and two - purple, red, and blue.

Three, four, maybe more.

Back, front, all around.

Representing you.

S. Gale

Roamy

Roamy is never here nor there.

No one can find her anywhere.

Roaming left and roaming right.

When you look, she's out of sight.

Roaming up and roaming down.

Man, the girl is all over town.

Flashing a smile on her face.

Then off she goes on her race.

Friends and family trying to trace.

Making calls to her place.

Roaming days and roaming nights.

Well, I guess you could say, she's quite liked.

Roamy is roaming again and again.

Going from family to friends.

There's just no end.

Love you from Roamy!

S. Gale

Wonder Why?

Have you ever wondered why; you look up in the sky so high?

And why the sun shines so bright?

Why the stars give off their light at night?

Did you ever look upon the clouds and wonder what it would be like above?

Have you ever imagined flying like a dove so high?

Have you ever wondered why the grass is green?

And why the spirits are unseen?

Did you ever wonder why you and I are here?

Take a look up there.

S. Gale

Dad

A dad is not always rough and tumble, nor beats.

Dads can be loving kind and sweet.

They say a man who shows his emotion is weak.

But a dad is a man, his emotions are meek.

This is the way they were designed from above.

Dad, you are cherished and loved.

You groom your children respectable like a bride.

Hold your head up high with pride.

S. Gale

She's Got No Hope

Living on dope, sniffing on coke.

Feel like you're in a tight rope and you're about to slit your throat.

NO HOPE?

Your baby's on the floor because you got no more, and everyone calls you a whore.

WHAT MORE?

Hope I've got no more if I bang my head on the floor.

Feel like running through the door.

My veins are squeezing thin with the blood that runs within.

The membranes in my brains are scattered all around as my body falls to the ground.

The screams are in my dreams, my floating body in the stream.

WHERE IS MY HOPE?

My dream to be that once lived in me.

Lord save me with your grace, take me to that place of embrace, where I can see your face.

Cover me with your wings that I may sing again.

With hope of your horizon that goes beyond the depth of my thoughts, that I may live again.

S. Gale

Keep Smiling

Keep smiling and walk away, to keep the peace for the day.

You never know the words that people say can impact us in so many different ways.

From your tone to your expression, words can do more harm than good.

So, keep smiling and walk away, to keep the peace for another day.

The heart expresses it in so many ways, it may be slight or even shy, bright eyed or wide.

Sometimes you might not know what to say.

Keep smiling and walk away.

S. Gale

Silent Mind (Dedicated Helen B.)

A silent mind is sitting wondering, is it a new beginning?

The mind of brilliance, transparent and sound.

Eyes that speak longing for change.

Inside that scrambling, things to be done and time that waits for NO one.

Choices conceived in the mind are often questioned.

Acceptance will be the thoughts that are real.

A voice inside that's still.

Millions of miles away.

Oh, silent mind deep in thought won't you SPEAK?

S. Gale

I Will Be (Dedicated to Cherry H.)

I will be that smile that says, "happy to see you" and the hugging arms that embrace too.

I will be your eyes to see the beauty that is near and your ears to hear the whistling sounds of things that are in the air.

I will be your hands to hold whatever you need, and your feet to walk at any speed.

The fingers that buckle your shoes and take them off too.

I will be your mouth to speak.

Unspoken words and stories untold.

I will be the laughter that rings through and the songs singing I love you.

I will be the intercessor when the burdens that you bear if you let me just be there.

I will be the tears that run down your cheeks when there are days you're feeling weak.

I will be the breath you cannot breathe and the pain your body feels.

I will be the friend you need in a heartbeat, that beats with love indeed.

S. Gale

Bills

Bills, bills every day, London, Canada, and the USA.

The postal is leaving on their way to bring the bills for you today.

What can you do? What can you say?

You better pay your bills right away.

Bills pon de left, bills pon de the right.

Bills all day and bills all night.

Bills uptown and bills downtown.

Bills have you running all around.

Don't know if you're going, don't know if you're coming.

Mortgage bill, visa bill, gas bill, water bill all kinds of bills.

Bills, bills, bills.

Bills from the east, bills from the west.

Bills, won't you give my brains a rest?

You've got me feeling such distress!

Can't even buy myself a new dress/vest.

Bills, bills every day the government set it up for you this way.

Driving you crazy before the day.

They'll cut your lights off and then they say, the bills will be coming for you to pay.

You're in the dark to find your way.

Bills, bills, everyday, London, Canada, and the USA.

We live in this life to be blessed.

So come on friends reduce the stress.

Before you know there's a pain on your chest.

And the doctors telling you to get some rest.

He writes a prescription from off his desk, and you'll be paying for the rest.

So, here's the answer to your "quest," pray to Jesus for your request and you'll be surely blessed.

S. Gale

Death

Often, we find one grieving over death.

The flesh that is still.

Pouring of tears and sorrow from deep down in the soul.

Family and friends, all dressed in black.

A casket shiny and dazzled up is carrying a loved one in the back.

Many minds are wondering where will that soul go?

You nor I know.

The preacher stands up in the church praying for one soul.

As we sit there both young and old, listening to his words.

The final ceremony is about to take place.

Everyone takes a stand.

Many weeping and wailing, holding each other's hands.

Watching as the casket lowers into the ground.

For as far as our knowledge and understanding, this is the end of death.

S. Gale

Moving On

When I move on, lay my body to rest.

But know that my spirit lives on.

Remember the smiles and the good times we shared.

Don't let me look down and see you weeping.

NO NOT ONE!

Remember my spirit lives on.

He who created me has called me home.

No more will I roam.

Know I am happy.

I hope I've made a difference in your lives - a gesture, a hug, maybe even a subtle word, or a smile.

I appreciate your respect.

Be kind to others.

Embrace with joy.

Keep love in your heart.

Peace!

S. Gale

Glow (In memories of Dad written for Mom)

I woke up this morning, the sun was shining, OH, what a beautiful glow!

I looked upon the mountains, the trees were orange, red, and yellow.

OH, what a beautiful glow!

The sky was bright, the breeze was blowing, the signs of autumn in the air.

Inside my heart grew weak.

Today will be the day when I take a ride by the side, where the lakes are silent, and the wind is still.

Nature is at its peace.

Walking down to the edge spreading the ashes of death.

Knowing that life was once within.

It is final.

Go in peace.

OH, what a beautiful glow.

S. Gale

Old Black Lady

Black lady, you are of my ancestors.

As I look at you what do I see?

Up in age, grey indeed!

Face so young and wrinkled free.

Black lady what do I see?

When I look in your eyes.

Your wandering eyes.

I see me in you and you in me.

As we are all one in a strange land.

Destined to be free.

Old Black lady.

S. Gale

Government Box

COVID-19 started in the year 2019, a virus unseen killing human beings.

Government screening, the world is screaming, first an epidemic then, a pandemic.

The world is shut in with panic, OMG, please don't let it be me!

From the glass and screens, families were seen for loved ones it's too late as they waved to their mates, high fevers praying believers on the other side waiting were receivers.

The numbers too great, hundreds and thousands in the crates.

Tick tock, racing up the clock, and there lies another government box.

S. Gale

TRINIDAD

Trinidad island in the sun.

A culture of music, food, and fun.

Mixed races, beautiful faces.

National events of colors, beauty at its best.

Day and night without any rest. Tell me that they're not blessed.

When the slaves of Indians and Blacks came, God's plans came into play.

A dougla race integrated.

Spices, rice's, all kind of nices with a masala twist.

Steel pan pinging and ponging away, 20th century music of today.

African drumbeat, spirit jumping out of their seat.

Shango Baptist all sort of Capitalist.

Government fighting for power, all working around the hour.

Workday, holiday, what "ya" say!

Man " gimae " "mae " pay.

Trini like a fete, soaking wet, dripping of sweat.

Calypso music playing, waistline and "Bumsee" swaying.

Dancing and prancing some tumbling down, yet they all stand as one.

Sea breeze and mango trees, paime on coconut leaves, grater cake, tamarind, and plum sauce.

Preparing for the main course. Roti how "yah " like it "bust up shot", curry dalpuri, dress up in "ya" sari.

Chutney, parang, all kind a slang.

"Ah" going round "de corner to come back " eh".

A lime it is not a fruit.

Family and friends liming in a group, what a hoot. Fiery people splendid in their mix.

Come to Trinidad if you want a natural fix.

B. Gale

Broken Hearted

A broken heart is what you gave me after all that we've been through.

Yes, we had our differences but wasn't I worth the fight to you?

Endless nights between cold sheets.

A lot of tears shed over you.

No longer willing to stay, I chose to walk away, from the hourglass you gave at the cost of my youth.

Time and attention was all I asked from you.

A dream of mine that couldn't come true.

A new world is what you introduced.

That unfortunately only belonged to you.

You neglected me, what can I say?

I deserve to be loved unconditionally.

Wouldn't you feel the same?

F. Gale

I'll Be Just Fine

After I lent my hand, I saw your back.

You asked, I gave, no questions asked.

You may cut off my hands, my heart still stands.

Mistaking kindness for weakness, you'll sink in wet sand.

You'll live with regret; cause trust me, I won't forget.

The victim roles you played, concerned about me you say?

Struggling from day to day, as I get back on track.

I reminisce back.

Bittersweet was our time.

Don't worry about me,

I'll be just fine.

F. Gale

My Masterpiece (Dedicated to Jayden)

Vibrant and young with energy for days.

When he was born, ten fingers, ten toes, skinny and long.

Weighing in at five pounds and five ounces my masterpiece was born.

At five years old my boy thinks he's grown.

Standing tall at three feet and four inches.

Eyes so bright he lights up my world.

A smile so big, it can't be ignored.

"Mommy am I masterpiece?" He asked.

I smiled and agreed.

Yes, you are!

You are my masterpiece.

F. Gale

Dear Son (Dedicated to Jayden)

Dear Son, I'm sorry.

I'm sorry if I broke your heart or shattered any of your dreams.

I promise you it was never my intention.

Not even a side effect in the main objective of things.

See, I made some choices and took a lot of chances.

Always keeping you in mind.

Now I feel like I'm failing.

All my plans have fallen through life's fine lines.

Never meant for you to be caught in the crossfire.

Custody battles and the back and forth.

Feeling tugged like you're the rope in Tug of War.

Or to witness the hatred between your mother and your father.

Screaming matches and late-night arguments.

Dear Son, I'm sorry.

I'm sorry we don't have the happy family that your heart desires.

Unfortunately, this isn't the fairy tale that you wished for.

This is mommy's real-life story and it's still being written.

And for that I'm sorry.

You have been beside me through it all.

The ups and downs.

From air mattresses to floors.

We've had our share of many options explored.

Still, our journey is far from the end.

I promise you son, better days will attend.

I've watched you sleep and shed my tears.

Silently wishing I could take away all your pains and fears.

Working hard day and night to make sure everything will be alright.

Fighting to ensure you have no needs.

Each night I drop down on my knees, saying a prayer.

Dear Lord, please continue to watch over us and keep him safe.

My work here is nowhere near complete.

Dear Son,

Please bear with me, I ask because I still have one last task.

I refuse to fail you.

F. Gale

Guardian Angel (Dedicated to Tasha)

You took me in when I had nowhere to go.

You spread your wings to shelter me from the cold.

You brought light into my darkest hours.

As my Guardian Angel, you protected me.

When I was down you picked me up.

Never judging me but advising me.

Reminding me of my worth.

As my Guardian Angel, you supported me.

We talked, we laughed, we shed many tears.

Growing stronger together after each breakthrough.

As my Guardian Angel, you loved me.

I will be forever grateful and will always love you.

F. Gale

No Regrets

To live each day in fear is a regret I refuse to share.

It takes courage to leave.

Yes, you left with good reasons don't ever forget.

You have your own life to live.

It takes strength to stand again.

This I know lives within.

F. Gale

Free

I know the feeling because I've been there before.

It's unfortunate cause the heart wants to soar.

Decisions are tough, that I can agree.

So, with this request, I ask you not to plead.

Please leave me be so I can be free.

You will always have a part of me.

F. Gale

Silly Rabbit

Silly Rabbit, your tricks are for kids!

Please stop acting like a little Bitch!

Please just say whatever it is, whatever it is that's stopping you from letting go of this.

This tit for tat shit is for little kids.

Something I thought we left to our eight-year-old kid.

You think you're hurting me?

Silly Rabbit!

You're only hurting him.

Actually, helping me by showing him your true colors that live within.

The main reason I left your ass in the very beginning.

The same reason why my emotions checked out the marriage years before I turned the ring in.

Silly Rabbit!

What grown-ass man requests money back from a child support check?

Won't spend time with him because I'm finally traveling?

Something you promised me but never made happened.

Like mother-like son will only babysit when I'm slaving.

Silly Rabbit, your tricks are for kids!

Please stop going through him, looking at me for a reaction.

Your petty miserable life no longer entices me.

Please stop playing the victim for others to see.

Throwing pity parties crying, "I don't know why she left me?"

Silly Rabbit, your tricks don't fool me.

F. Gale

Is This What You Call an Apology?

Another night, another fight.

As we begin to argue.

Screaming at each other.

Clearly not listening to one another.

Words are thrown.

Names are called.

Feelings are hurt.

Tears are shed.

I walk away to escape this emotional blood battle.

Away from you I go and lay down.

Cold and wet from the pool of water that left from my eyes.

Some time has passed.

Crick crack, the door opens.

Too mad to turn around.

Jump at the touch of your hand rubbing on my skin.

Chills travel down my legs and up my inner thighs as your fingers lead the way to my inner temple.

Too hurt to speak I tighten my thighs hoping you can read the NOT WELCOME sign!

But you don't as you flip my body letting me know what's about to take place.

As you plant a kiss I turn and wish this isn't about to happen.

Your clothes come off and I fight to keep mine on.

You try then stop as you forcefully pull my panties to the side.

The pool gets deeper as you begin to enter.

I lay in disgust, crying to myself.

How could this be from a man who claims to love me?

Being raped by my mate?

Is this truly my fate?

I lay still as could be awaiting the end to come.

Is this what you call an apology?

F. Gale

Did I Fight the Right Battle? (Dedicated to Jayden)

I am stronger beyond your imagination.

Nowhere near as weak as I may seem.

Although I may smile with my eyes.

I truly see the lies that lay inside of your desires.

As much as you may want to break me down.

I refuse to lay upon that ground.

Refuse to be left weak with regret.

Wondering on what could have been.

What might have been?

Did I choose to fight the right battle?

Instead of sitting here going back and forth like a baby's rattle.

Over what is that is, my freedom at hand.

As hard as it may be, to wake up with no one next to me.

To make the effort to role-play each day.

Pretending to be Superwoman just to put a smile on his precious face.

When all I want to do is crawl back into bed.

To be left alone.

It's that innocent smile that I help create.

That keeps me going and reminds me each day.

Yes, I fought the right battle!

F. Gale

Ignorance

You said you would help me in any way you can.

Yet you don't.

Instead, you make things as difficult as you can.

Do you wonder why I am the way I am?

If you knew me, you would know.

Sad thing is you don't.

Here alone, I am.

But to you, who gives a damn?

Your pride and ignorance won't allow you to see just how great our friendship could be.

You said you tried but we both know that's a lie!

My love is worth much more than the half a heart you were giving me.

You want to get along you say?

Show some respect and a little love.

It goes a long way.

Hate is love and love is hate.

Please stop making every little thing a debate.

Yes, we both made some mistakes.

However, bringing them up isn't worth the headaches.

F. Gale

Invisible signs

Another lonely night.

Another disappointment.

Always something keeping us apart.

Preventing us from ever getting back to our moment.

Beginning to think that's a sign.

Life's been trying to show me who you are this entire time.

The one with nothing but empty words and broken promises.

Feels like a never-ending cycle.

Creating cramps in my chest.

Which prevents that beat in my heart to ever love or trust again.

Just when I thought I found the one.

Here, life comes with another warning.

That you may not be the one who I've been waiting for this entire time.

Pay attention those invisible signs!

F. Gale

Loves Journey

I never thought I could or would ever love again.

Then you came into my life unexpected and unplanned.

Bringing light into my dark days and life into my heart.

You've unwillingly taken over my thoughts and are missed every moment we spend apart.

The beauty of a broken heart is that when it rebuilds it's much stronger to love that much harder.

I have you to thank for reminding me of such.

Whatever journey life has awaiting me, I no longer shy away; but am willing to take it on at the thought of you next to me.

F. Gale

Fear of Failure (Dedicated to Jayden)

I always said I'd rather struggle alone and be happy than live in misery with someone else.

These days I find myself torn, for I never expected to be in the predicament that I find myself in.

Feeling helpless and lost.

Broke down and worn.

Fighting to raise a boy into a man, on my very own.

At times I feel like I'm losing my grip.

Feels like I'm standing on the edge of a cliff.

Speaking out loud but not being heard.

Grasping for air, fighting to breathe.

Taking a step forward to only be pushed ten steps back.

This pain in my chest leaves me exhausted and weak.

Some nights I lay in bed drenched in a pool from tears that have escaped me uncontrollably.

My biggest fear is failure.

I say my prayer before I sleep,

Please Lord don't let me fail him.

F. Gale

Promise Me

If I die tomorrow promise me one thing.

The love we make today will be everlasting.

Not just in your mind but your body, heart, and soul.

For today I want you to look at me like you never have before.

See me completely, entirely from head to toe.

Touch my heart with laughter, till it overflows.

Make it flutter like a butterfly. Make it skip a beat or two.

So every time your heart skips a beat, you'll remember me too.

Make today about us, our love, and our time.

For if today is the last, I want you to be all mine.

As we lay hand in hand reminiscing about our time.

Looking back at our history.

The creation of our love story.

With all my heart I request this one last thing.

Please promise me you'll kiss me as if it's our first.

You'll touch me as if it's our last, and that the love we make today will forever last.

Promise me.

F. Gale

Impatiently Waiting

As I lay in bed at night tossing and turning,

the cold air between the sheets is missing the warmth from your body.

Stretching out wishing you were here.

Yearning the touch of your skin pressed up against mine.

My mind reminiscing back to the last time.

I seductively searched for your groin with my behind.

There was no doubt I would find it.

Just a matter of time for a chance to unwind.

Your absence leaving my hands in a bind.

Rubbing myself from my breast to my insides.

I rolled my head back and close my eyes.

Impatiently waiting until the next time.

F. Gale

Love Is Out the Door

It feels as though my heart has lost the will to love.

See I no longer look at love like I once did before.

Been broken and hurt too many times to restore.

I've accepted the fact that love doesn't live here anymore.

Tired of broken promises, high hopes, and empty dreams.

The meaningless words, the lies, and the games.

You break once you rebuild stronger than before.

You break twice you catch the lessons that you missed the first time.

After the third broken heart, love is out the door.

F. Gale

Love Got Me

Love hasn't been too good to me.

I always end up with a heavy heart.

See, when I love, I love hard.

Causing the hurt to be that much more.

Nothing within my reach I won't do.

Leaves the pain forever lingering.

Never expecting it could happen again.

These feelings I'm feeling now seem foreign.

I'm thinking love has tricked me again.

For the man I love says he loves me.

But his behavior says differently.

Saying those three words are meaningless without the actions to support.

Blinded by what I want to see.

I forgive and let be.

Feels like I'm a well-hidden secret these days.

That only he can keep.

God damn love has gotten me again.

Feel like a fool lost inside his web of lies.

I close my eyes and say a prayer.

Wishing God would make me see more clearly.

I pray that his heart truly loves mine and if it doesn't,

God damn, please stop wasting my time.

F. Gale

Mistaken Words

This pain in my chest won't leave just yet.

As thoughts of you overflow in my head.

Mistaken words that left my breath, had you fall back.

Leaving our love for dead.

Missing you with every breath I take.

From foolish words that escaped.

That unfortunately can never be erased.

Mourning as I lay us to rest.

These words that I said haunt me as if spoken from the dead.

Spoken out of disappointment, hurt, and confusion.

Causing me to lose focus but just for one moment.

Shed many tears of the mere thought of you fading out of my existence.

Can no longer bear the punishment of your silent ways.

I can apologize to you each and every day.

However, these words I say can never truly express the love my heart feels for you in so many ways.

This pain in my chest won't leave just yet from mistaken words that left my breath.

F. Gale

My Fault

You drive this wild desire inside.

Something I have never felt before.

Except, the way you treat me is bad for my health.

You see my fault is always wanting to help.

With you, I saw the good that no one else could see.

Saw the pain that you carried in your chest.

Making it hard for you to ever love someone else.

The anger and frustration from having the cards you were dealt.

You see my fault is always wanting to help.

I wanted to bring that good out when you couldn't yourself.

Wanting to take away the pain that you held in your chest.

Wanting to help you lay your past to rest.

By loving you whole heartily and no one else.

To show you it's ok, you can trust and love again.

Wanting to give you a new deck of cards and shuffle them again and again.

You see my fault is always wanting to help.

You see, I realized I can't help you if you won't help yourself.

F. Gale

BFF

I have one true best friend in this world.

That sticks with me through thick and thin.

I guarantee you she will be with me to the very end.

I never have to call her because she's always there when I need her most.

Like a ghost, she works in mysterious ways.

Anyone screws me over, won't be able to surrender.

Always makes sure they get what they deserve.

Never failing to even the score.

She's truly a bitch in her ways, as many of you would say.

Please believe I do my part to keep peace whenever we're apart.

This is one friend I refuse to piss off.

Cause when she strikes back, all bets are off.

What goes around, comes around, and she flies first class.

I make sure I treat others with respect.

Never do to others what I wouldn't want done back.

That's why I can proudly say she will never be looking for me someday.

Let me stop being rude and properly introduce.

My best friend for life is Karma.

Now isn't that a Bitch!

F. Gale

New Feelings

Confusion is far from these emotions I'm feeling.

The ability to dream again after feeling like dreaming wasn't part of my existence.

Feels like a breath of fresh air.

Amazing how this unfamiliar attraction feels so comfortable.

No fears lie here.

Just pure desire and excitement.

My only concern is that you no longer hurt from the past but embrace the future.

Realize your worth and ignore those who don't.

Not trying to sound harsh love, but I've had my share of broken hearts.

Understanding that time is what you need.

I'm willing to turn over your hourglass as many times as you please.

My patience is nowhere near weary.

Especially when I see that beautiful smile.

My light at the end of the tunnel.

Confusion is far from these emotions I'm feeling.

Thankful for this new beginning.

F. Gale

Won't Let You

Sometimes I feel like I've failed him.

His father swears he's doing right by him.

All my efforts, blood, sweat, and tears don't amount to anything?

A few harsh words and you swear you're about something.

How can it be, eight days a month can ever compare to the time I spend with him?

You can't take nothing from me!

Not my love, passion, or the air I breathe.

I've been doing me!

Long before you could ever see.

Life without you is pure self-indulgent!

You fail to see that he is my destiny, my pride, my joy, my reason for being!

No, you can take that away from me.

No matter how much better you think you are than me.

I know that he loves me.

He relies, depends, and even looks up to me.

So no matter what you say to me, you will never take that from me.

I no longer need your validation for the fantastic mother I'm being.

Screw you and all your negativity.

I won't let you keep harassing me.

Refuse to let you still control me.

This power you had to infuse your misery into me, I now declare my history.

Don't say nothing to me.

Your words aren't worth my energy.

No, I won't let you ruin my freedom.

I know I will always do right by him.

F. Gale

Stagnant

I lost all control.

Somewhere down this lonely road.

I'm stuck and can't move.

Screaming for help and can't be heard.

I've lost the greatest love that my heart will ever know.

Amazing how the world works.

You want those that don't want you.

The ones that want you, you don't want.

I wish we met at another time.

When you were meant to be mine.

Unfortunately, nothing happens before its time.

I envisioned us growing old together.

A lifetime filled with love and laughter.

Next to one another until our last breath.

I guess you were never meant to be mine in this lifetime.

All I can do is shed a few tears.

As my heart bleeds in sorrow, for we no longer have any more tomorrows.

F. Gale

Hanging on by A Thread

I'm dying a very slow and painful death.

Eyes drowning in tears.

Bloodshed from my heart.

I no longer know what to do.

Life has lost all meaning without you.

Love has left this empty feeling, like a shell shooting through the barrel.

I need to escape the endless thought of you and I, but I can't!

I close my eyes at night wishing that this dream would come true.

For the nightmares of not being enough to conclude.

To wake up one day and see that I too, can be loved just as much as I once loved you.

Is it true?

See these days I'm losing all hope.

Holding on as tight as I can to the end of the rope.

As I dare myself to be brave enough to just let go.

It's just a matter of time till death becomes my throne.

They say time heals all wounds, but no matter how much time passes I'm still missing you.

True my love doesn't come easy.

It's not so easy to vanish away.

So, unless love comes knocking.

Love will see me morn yet another day.

F. Gale

Let's Play

You broaden my horizons in more ways than one.

These little mental mind games I see, they're not just for fun.

Got my mind spinning.

Have me even calculating.

Had to take a step back to focus on the hidden meanings.

Some love lasts a minute, others a lifetime.

Once caught up, it becomes your lifestyle.

From afar things look gravy.

But deep inside things are actually flaky.

Kneeled down I pray for a cleanse.

Knowing that tomorrow isn't always in our fortune.

They say let it go, if it's meant to be it will return.

So, until then, I'll continue to play.

Patiently waiting for our day.

F. Gale

My Misconception

I thought love was this misconception that no longer exists in my world.

Always giving 100%

Only receiving 10%

Far from my vision of my true love, you entered into my world.

Swept me off my feet, completely throwing me off guard.

Yet pulling me into sync.

Can now see clearly but can't explain my thoughts.

Torn between my head and my heart.

One says stay, the other yells STOP!

You've totally and completely consumed my thoughts.

From our first kiss, you have my head spent.

Impatiently waiting for the next.

Waking up this morning I realize love is no longer this misconception, but a possibility in my future.

F. Gale

I'm Looking For

I'm looking for a true Ride or Die.

Someone like myself.

Loyal to the end.

Who wants nothing more than to be my best friend.

Puts a smile on my face.

Knows how to kiss me in the right place.

Can make me laugh all day.

Share stories all night.

Be my rock when I'm weak.

Got my back when I need.

Show me the way when I can't see.

Yet someone who isn't me.

Someone who compliments me and challenges me, all in the same speech.

Who gets me without wanting to change me.

No need to explain the way I think.

I'm looking for peace and happiness till our last breath.

I'm looking for unconditional love with no rules attached.

No batteries needed.

No need for a way out.

Our time spent is never enough.

I'm looking for the love of my life.

A fairy tale ending that rarely exists.

Someone to save me from my lonely existence.

I pray for God to send him my way.

These days he seems to be further and further away.

Lord, please tell me he's on his way.

F. Gale

Time Will Tell

You asked to hear my story, from beginning to the end.

Trust me there's no need to rush.

By the looks of things, our time will never end.

We'll have plenty nights for pillow talk.

Many days to joke and play around.

I'll share my story tale by tale, unfiltered from here on out.

Sharing the written and my many dreams.

My tears will explain my secrets and fears.

My laughter will unfold my pleasures and joy.

Maybe just maybe you'll stick around to help fill in what's unwritten.

All depends on if you like what I have to say.

Only time will tell.

F. Gale

Lowered Eyes

You may not be able to see my eyes, but don't worry I see you.

May not be telling me the truth, but no worries I hear you.

May not tell me your thoughts, but don't worry I feel you.

See I've been there before.

Loved till it hurts, to be left and be hurt even more.

Left behind to unwind the damage from the one that stole your heart.

I've also pushed those away that said they cared.

Not trusting the words that slipped through their mouths.

Testing their action and comparing them to the ones I've lost.

So, when you see me quiet with my head bowed don't think I don't see you.

I see you.

When you see me quiet and I don't speak, don't think I don't hear you.

I hear you and most definitely feel you.

My eyes are lowered.

I can't endure the pain to see you that way.

I've been there before.

My head is bowed in a silent prayer to relieve you from the pain.

F. Gale

Save Me

Dear Lord, please save me.

I'm drowning in sorrow.

Have shed enough tears over the years, that I'm no longer willing to beg or borrow.

I dread to see tomorrow.

Heartache after headaches.

Please, Lord, I'm asking for a break.

Please let the sunshine my way.

Make this never-ending storm go away.

Too tired to work, too broke to quit.

All the work I've done, yet still standing at square one.

What happened to the balance, between good and evil?

These days it feels like the devil is two steps ahead of your plan.

I'm chained down with no way out.

Every attempt I make just doesn't pan out.

I refuse to accept this to be true.

That's why I'm on my knees and continue to turn your way.

Please Lord, save me.

F. Gale

Can't Breathe

I can't breathe.

I'm suffocating.

The walls around me, won't stop caving in.

All opportunities keep turning into dead ends.

So-called friends who claim, "I got you," nowhere to be found.

When I stand lost in a crowd.

Left alone to drown.

I can't breathe.

The oxygen no longer passing through my lungs.

People claim they want to help you when it's only themselves they're looking out for.

I'm suffocating.

Trapped inside with no way out.

Stuck to failure like it was all planned out.

Every effort tired, every leaf turned over.

In the end, all efforts don't seem to matter.

Success has turned its back on me.

Not once or twice but multiple times over.

So often I'm left with sore shoulders.

Tired beyond exhaustion from carrying this weight on my shoulders.

As I continue to lack in air, running in circles as I come near to my fear.

The walls continue to cave in.

I gasp for my last breath.

No more strength to fight it.

That's it! I give in!

F. Gale

Hercules Cried (Dedicated to My Brother)

I saw Hercules cry today.

I was shocked and scared.

How can a man so strong just burst into tears?

Do I ignore him and pretend not to see?

Or wrap my arms around him?

Tell him I love him and that it will be ok, whatever it is that made him feel this way.

My heart crumbles at the sight of the water drops strolling down his cheek.

I need to make this right and take away his pain.

Which Bitch is it that caused it to rain?

Stealing precious time from us.

Dominating his thoughts, controlling his heart.

Creating the day, I thought I would never see.

My lonely brother no longer wanting to breathe.

I swear I will not rest or be at ease, until the water stops running and his heart is at peace.

How dare you abuse the kindness of his heart?

Stomping on it till it bleeds.

For your sake and mine, I pray I never have to see Hercules cry again.

F. Gale

Empty Vessel

My body feels like an empty vessel.

Standing here alone feels like my soul has escaped, already on the roam.

But why?

Why do I feel like life is passing me by?

Silent words escape my mouth, as they sit unheard.

Meaningless thoughts fill my head unable to be shared.

Am I better off dead?

Time will tell, I guess?

I see happiness swarming around me, yet I can't grasp it.

Life won't allow me to experience it.

Won't allow me to hold onto it.

Only teases me with happy moments with a short life span.

An empty vessel, I am.

F. Gale

This Can't Be Life

This can't be life.

Waking up every morning dreading the day that has just begun.

Far from ungrateful that I've been blessed with another day.

A day that wasn't promised, but Lord there has to be more.

More than working a 9-5 barely getting home in time.

No time to cook or spend with the one reason I do all this for.

Feeling stuck.

Hate my job but can't afford to quit or go back to school.

This can't be the example I'll be leaving behind.

Slave all day then cry all night.

Wondering when it will be my time?

To shine or be blessed, either one that will give me the chance to rest.

Tired of helping others when I need help myself.

I keep giving and continue to go without.

Looking back at life like what the hell have I done?

All these years I've worked hard and have nothing to show.

I have given until my hands have bled.

This can't be life.

Working harder than the person sitting next to me making less because I'm not white.

All my dreams shot down by my reality.

Places I wanted to go no longer an option.

Just somewhere I can only wish to explore.

Pretending to be stronger than I am is exhausting.

Fighting to shelter him from my fears and the wear and tears I've endured.

Dear Lord, this can't be life.

F. Gale

Lights Camera Action

People say their life is a movie.

I say mine is a Broadway show.

There are no lies, nowhere to hide, this shit is live.

The shit I've been through.

From eighteen I left home.

From Canada to NYC, I went.

Young, dumb, and thought I was in love.

Had no family around I didn't even look back.

Thinking I'm grown at eighteen I married a Jamaican man.

By twenty we bought a house I never called home.

Connecticut here I roam.

Further away from any friends I made.

Twenty-one, I gave birth to my son.

Ready or not motherhood here I come.

Twenty-two, I decide to go back to school.

Fight to juggle a newborn, two jobs, school, and a home.

Twenty-six, I was fed up, had way more than enough.

No wife should ever have to beg for her husband's touch.

Left my marriage and my house.

Swore I would never settle or sacrifice myself for anyone else.

Determined to have my son see his mother live happily.

I found myself back in New York City.

Jobless and homeless, refused to miss his first day of school.

Stayed in hotels alone with whatever I saved up.

Blessed by an ex-sister-in-law.

The ex-wives club was made.

You see, both of us divorced the brothers from Jamaica West Indies.

Funny how life works you see.

Called a living room my home.

Slept on an air mattress for a year.

Please believe I was happy as could be.

Truly blessed, I could never forget, question, or complain, but excited for the change.

My son saw the way mommy hustled every day.

Twenty-eight was my year I landed on my feet.

Found a place to call my own.

Got a career to take care of our home.

Proud of the woman I've become.

My son now smiles when he can say,

"Mommy I love you! I'm happy we're home!"

I tend to laugh when I hear them say, "Their life is a movie." cause mine's a Broadway show.

A snapshot into my journey.

Not to mention, depression, heartbreaks, and many struggles I endured along the way.

People say their life is a movie, I say mine's a Broadway show.

F. Gale

Beat

Beat like the drummer man's drum.

This single mother shit ain't just for anyone.

Hats off to those who have more than one.

All the dreams we said goodbye to.

Romantic nights we no longer get to.

Endless hours we slave.

The many second chances we gave.

Not to mention extremely underpaid.

Fighting each day to provide a better tomorrow than our yesterdays.

Beat like the steel pan drum.

This single mother shit ain't just for anyone.

Scrapping to make ends meet.

Searching the kitchen and all its cabinet draws hoping some food would appear
that wasn't there before.

Pretending that everything is okay.

Just so they don't see our hurt and pain.
As we calculate which bill to pay.

Continue to go without just to ensure they have.

The list can go on forever but FUCK it. I'm beat!

F. Gale

Thinking of you (In memories of N. Gale)

As I think of my love, the one who died.

The tears fall from my eyes.

I still cannot believe he's gone.

I know he will always be around.

I sit in the living room by myself.

I feel the sadness and the tears.

Life without him is hard, you know.

I am so sorry he had to go.

It was his time to go on home.

That's why I'm left here all alone.

Goodbye my love, I have to say.

Until we meet again someday.

 B. Gale

46546479R00051